TWO TRUTHS
ONE WORLD

STEVE RICHARDSON

The moral rights of the author are asserted.

All rights reserved. No part of this book may be reproduced by any mechanical, photographic or electronic process, or in the form of a phonographic recording nor may be stored in a retrieval system, transmitted or otherwise be copied for public or private use, other than for 'fair use' as brief quotations embodied in articles and reviews, without prior written permission of the publisher.

Although every precaution has been taken in preparing this book, the publisher and author assume no responsibility for errors or omissions. Neither is any liability assumed for damages resulting from the use of information contained herein.

Copyright © 2024 Steve Richardson

All rights reserved.

FOR MY

Children
Ancestors
Guides
Teachers

	Introduction	vi
1	Fear and Ego	1
2	Choice and Control	13
3	Learn To Love	21
4	Love To Learn	47
5	One World	66
6	Final Words	77
7	Learn To Love Ideas	82
8	Love To Learn Ideas	84
9	Workshops	82

INTRODUCTION

Imagine, for a moment, if, just like Aladdin, a genie appeared and offered you three wishes. What would be your three wishes?

Perhaps you might reach for the obvious – lots of money. With an abundance of confirmed wealth, you might consider for your next wish how you might benefit the lives of those in your family – long lives, excellent health, or perhaps healing a long-suffering ailment.

And then, for your final wish, you might turn your newfound benevolence upon humanity. Insist on world peace, cure all the major diseases known to man or abolish poverty.

And I've noticed that most people follow the above pattern whenever I pose the three-wish question.

But what if I told you that you don't need three wishes? Contained within the Two Truths is the remedy to all that ails humanity.

Perhaps not in the time span or the way people might want, but if lived fully, the Two Truths would fulfil the wishes and dreams of many, if not all, people on Earth.

I know, it's a huge claim. But it's a claim I'm happy to stand by, and as you progress through the book, you'll see why.

I experienced an intellectual and emotional tussle when I started writing this little volume.

It wasn't an existential mountain with which I was climbing. It was the challenge of squaring the fact that two simple truths, so innate to humankind, are being diluted at best and, at worst, forgotten by many.

And I include myself. Historically, whenever I have forgotten, avoided or misused the Two Truths, I have made substantial life errors, hurt people and stagnated my development.

So, in the same way, nature fills a vacuum; the absence of The Two Truths in our world has introduced much that hurts our planet and humanity. As a species, we've lost our way a little – and some might say a lot.

This understanding of the current state of the human condition is separate from the many beautiful and meaningful things people do for the benefit of others worldwide.

However, it is a realisation that despite the goodness that exists, too many still feel lonely, unloved, unheard, judged, separated, and dismissed.

Sadly, we live in a world where many lack self-belief, self-esteem, happiness, and purpose. Perhaps most tragically, too many individuals are running on empty when it comes to self-love. But this woeful state of affairs does not have to be the case.

There are so many instances when individuals and groups make a difference, and when this happens (*and in every case, by the way*), it starts with someone, somewhere, activating one or both of the Two Truths.

These heroes make incremental gains for humanity - one building block at a time.

You hear of them in families, communities, work, and social groups. By embracing the Two Truths, they make people think and act differently.

They get people to think and act beyond the self, to appreciate that we are all connected by our humanity.

They contribute not just in word and deed but also by fostering a change in consciousness by getting us to reconnect with the Two Truths. Better still *(is there anything better?),* these extraordinary individuals help shift our energy and habits from the habitual status quo.

They inspire and encourage us to be more positive, kinder, and loving to ourselves. Because we are beings of energy and light, this shift in energy matters.

Indeed, our energy and interconnectivity to the Universe and each other are an integral part of living the Two Truths. I've shown how that connection works in this little volume.

The Two Truths are vital to achieving peace and collective harmony on our planet. They are as intrinsic to our individual and collective well-being and survival as the planet we live on and the air we breathe.

Our connection to the Two Truths is powerful and undeniable. Each truth has its unique purpose, and if nurtured and lived, it helps us grow towards the true measure expected of our creation.

Sadly, when the Two Truths are absent in a person's life – you will see unhappiness and a lack of purpose.

Equally, if the Two Truths are absent in a community, family or group, you will see chaos, dissatisfaction, and disharmony.

However, when people embrace the Two Truths, I have seen relationships repair and flourish, self-confidence grow, trauma heal, self-image restore, and creativity set free.

And importantly, individuals passionately pursue their life purpose.

I hope that by the time you reach the end of this book, you will feel moved to embrace the Two Truths deeply into your life. Thereafter, my dearest wish is that you inspire and encourage others to do the same.

I hope you enjoy what follows.

Steve

CHAPTER 1
Fear and Ego

I have Two Truths I would like to share with you. If you embrace them, they will simplify how you live your life.

Indeed, let me go further and be bolder. Placing these Two Truths at the centre of your life will make you happier, healthier, more content, braver, hugely optimistic and certainly more confident than you can imagine.

That said, please take my word that I am not encouraging you to start something unattainable. These two truths have been proven to transform people's lives and can provide a much-needed balm for much of what ails our world.

However, before we arrive at that blessed condition, I wish to highlight two factors in our personal lives that are guaranteed to sabotage our best endeavours to live the Two Truths.

These two miscreants influence humankind to various degrees, with wide-ranging personal, community, family and national consequences.

They are two features of our human condition: variously dressed up to excuse behaviours, avoiding taking responsibility and insisting one's way is the only way.

They can happily operate individually or in harmony.

Distorted perceptions, dogma, myopic belief systems, analysis paralysis, risk aversion, groupthink, and ignorance are their bread and butter.

We can experience these two personality quirks daily in various ways, often subtle and innocuous. They influence decisions at work and home, and they readily inform prejudice and generate hard-wired and harmful belief systems.

They are, if you haven't guessed, fear and ego.

These two intertwined traits, fear and ego, can profoundly impact our personal lives. They can erode our self-confidence, limit our experiences and opportunities, and even prevent us from healing past wounds. These traits can also be traced back to the roots of major societal issues like war, poverty, and racism.

One might say conflict of any nature starts with these divisive personality flaws.

EGO

The Latin root meaning of ego is I - or, in other words, the self, that which feels, acts or thinks.

Most of us will have used various terms associated with ego during our lifetime, such as ego trip, inflated ego, egotism, ego mania, or alter ego. Or perhaps, more rarely, egoless.

The question is not how you respond toward your ego but only what you believe you are.

Sigmund Freud popularised the term within the psychology field, slowly infiltrating the social spectrum. Of course, Freud used ego in association with the human psychological identities of the id and the super-ego. So, loosely speaking, we can define the three as:

The id: Is a part of the unconscious that contains all our urges and impulses, including the libido. The id operates on the pleasure principle, that every unconscious wishful impulse should be satisfied immediately, regardless of the consequences.

The ego: The ego is the part of the id modified by the external world's direct influence.

The super-ego: The super-ego consists of two systems: The conscience and the ideal self.

The conscience is the inner voice that tells us when we have done something intuitively wrong or out of harmony with what is considered acceptable.

The super-ego operates on the morality principle and motivates us to behave in a socially responsible and acceptable manner.

The three parts of our ego are embarking on a daily struggle to become dominant. Compounding matters, the ego initiates defence mechanisms to react to situations with negative emotions.

When facets of the id make incursions into consciousness, the ego is prone to counterattack by deploying defence mechanisms. After all, *the ego fears nothing more than inferiority or to be ignored.*

These defence mechanisms may prove useful or detrimental depending on how they are used. The most common defence mechanisms are:

Denial
Refuse to accept reality or facts.

Repression
Unconsciously choosing to hide painful memories or irrational beliefs in hopes of forgetting them entirely.

Projection
Misattributing feelings upon another person.

Displacement
Directing strong emotions and frustrations toward a person or object that doesn't feel threatening.

Regression
Unconsciously escaping to an earlier stage of development.

Rationalisation
Explaining undesirable behaviours based on your generated set of facts.

Sublimation
Redirecting strong emotions or feelings into an object or activity that is appropriate and safe.

Compartmentalisation
Separating your life into independent sectors in a way to protect many elements of it.

Reaction formation
Recognising how you feel, but choosing to behave in the opposite manner of your instincts.

Intellectualisation
Removing all emotion from your responses and instead focus on quantitative facts.

Of course, when some of these defence mechanisms are negatively used or combined, we see pride, arrogance, selfishness, dogma, entitlement, blame, prejudice, bending the truth or blatantly ignoring it.

These traits are common for those in power who profess to know what is best for the masses while safeguarding their power, status, influence, or money.

Additionally, you will see a narrowing and absence of learning and listening and, in some cases, a complete lack of understanding, compassion, and empathy.

I think Albert Einstein understood this fully when he said, "*Whoever undertakes to set himself up as a judge in the field of truth and knowledge is shipwrecked by the laughter of the gods.*"

When a scientist, physicist, priest, academic, politician, academic, or doctor insists they possess the absolute truth about a particular idea, belief, or dogma, we can be assured that the ego is flourishing, and curiosity and compromise are being ignored.

To combat being seduced by those who zealously expound their particular agenda, it is vital that our ego possesses a well-developed and informed scepticism that nurtures an open mind. A mind that explores with curiosity, without fear, and without prejudice that which is not known or even believed by others.

For example, in the 1940s - 1950s, it was a common occurrence in the United States for radio stations to report and openly discuss UFO sightings with their listeners. In the 1960s, this happy state changed.

The *'industrial military complex'*, as identified by President Eisenhower, decided that the public must see UFOs as a hoax based on camera tricks, weather phenomena, light anomalies, too much beer or just an individual insufficiently smart enough to understand what was seen.

Consequently, despite *Operation Blue Book* and countless sightings and reports by people worldwide, pseudo-sceptics continue to ridicule and peddle their subjective opinions on the matter - actively helped by close-lipped governments.

For more information on this matter, one can review Dr. Stephen Greer's lifetime work, particularly The Disclosure Project.

Notwithstanding, we should not allow the harmful social norms of ego to steer us away from what a healthy ego represents. A healthy, cultivated, regulated and mature ego fights for what we profoundly believe - in a sense, it is our inner spirit.

We must learn by error, course correction and endeavour to appreciate the need to move beyond the emotional and dogmatic excesses demanded of the fragile ego. We do this by harnessing the power of the Two Truths.

FEAR

In the film After Earth, Will Smith's character turns to his son and says, "*The only place that fear can exist is in our thoughts of the future. Do not misunderstand me; danger is real, but fear is a choice.*"

I wonder if you subscribe to the sentiment that fear, is a choice.

If the movie character's premise is correct, that fear is a future yet unrealised destination, what do we think is being accomplished by being fearful now? After all, we have no control over the future—although we often think this is the case.

After all, how often have you worried about a dilemma and inserted the worst possible outcome? Fear has the unnerving ability to keep us rooted to the spot or fleeing for refuge. It is an emotional mechanism that transforms a subjective and unwritten future into an incontrovertible reality.

Fear is only as deep as the mind allows.

And the longer fear embeds into your life, the longer it influences your daily reality into a kaleidoscope of anxiety, distress, insomnia, stress and a sense of hopelessness.

At its core, fear is about loss - the idea is that the future will change for the worse. It is as though the depth of attachment to current circumstances is so deep that any changes appear catastrophic at worst and, at best - highly undesirable.

Attachments, a universal human experience, can become fertile ground for fear. The longer we hold onto them, the deeper the fear of losing them becomes.

This fear of loss can induce a wide range of behaviours, including features of control, deceit, selfishness, denial, and obsession.

Here are a few contemporary examples of attachment:

- Politicians and their power and influence
- A neighbour and their parking space
- A social media influencer and their followers
- A worker and their job security
- A model and their looks

Anything that generates fear or any perception of loss, harms individuals, families, communities, and nations.

In Buddhist philosophy, attachment is seen as a source of suffering and a hindrance to personal growth. The Sanskrit word upādāna further expands the meaning to grasping or clinging.

This grasping or clinging is a faulty thought construction about reality because we live in a world where change is inevitable. It is an immutable law that everything is in transition.

For example, in war-torn countries, families tragically see their homes destroyed daily. Suddenly, their attachment to a building they called home is replaced by the need to find something else to shelter and protect the family. Necessity becomes the author of invention.

In these and similar situations, fear converts into action, and action turns into adaptability and resilience - a central strength of humankind when it is needed. Fear is overcome and a different choice is made.

These situations are heart-breaking, and war and conflict should never happen. Yet, families in these situations adapt and overcome because choices have to be made, and these choices are made despite fear.

What initially seems an unthinkable fear becomes a new reality with which they must live.

"Whoever can see through fear will always be safe.

The underlying principle of attachment to the material or the immaterial confirms it is a futile exercise. Fundamentally, job redundancies will happen, loved ones will die, romances will end, beliefs will be unseated, power will disappear, influence will vanish, looks will fail, and possessions will be lost.

There is a clear association between stress and the existential fear of losing anything considered important in life, no matter how superficial. The more individuals cling and grasp to avoid enforced change, the greater the stress.

There is a Buddhist story that illustrates the runaway power of fear.

'A priest in the countryside walks down a lane that meanders towards the horizon. It is a hot summer's day with little wind and no shade from the sun's heat. In the distance, the priest sees a rising cloud of dust.

As the dust cloud approaches, he sees a horse with a rider galloping down the lane. As the horse draws closer, it becomes evident to the priest that he must step to the side of the lane; otherwise, the horse may trample him.

As the horse nears the priest, he shouts to the rider, "Where are you going?"

The rider yells, "I don't know - ask the horse."

The story highlights that fear is a dangerous emotion that can take hold of us and lead us down a path with no clear goal or end. Fear has no destination or rationale because it is a product of our imagination.

Thus, the map is not the territory!

Sustained and unregulated fear has one destination: poor mental, physical, and emotional health.

Fear floods our bodies with stress hormones that negatively impact our immune system, hinder cellular growth, bring toxicity to gut health, disrupt our sleep, wreck our diet, and destroy emotional and mental well-being.

Being afraid of anything, means you acknowledge its power to hurt you.

Equally, it is essential to remember that attachment and fear are members of the same destructive family. If you are convinced (*attached*) that the worst will happen, you automatically shut down options and remove action.

The more profound the conviction (attachment), the greater the fear and the more despair and unhappiness one feels.

Whenever you are afraid, it is a sure sign that you have allowed your mind to miscreate an outcome; that is, you have not allowed your higher self to guide the fear into a rational place. When you are fearful, you have willed wrongly.

You have willingly miscreated an outcome - not created a reality!

We must remember that fear is a choice. We have control over fear no matter how difficult it seems. Yes, it requires a change of perspective, but the only person who can completely control fear is ourselves.

CHAPTER 2
Choice and Control

Choice is an integral part of life. Our choices show to ourselves and others what is important to us. They offer gateways into what gives meaning to our lives.

Unfortunately, some choices tend to offer the wrong meaning to our lives.

For example, our work ethic, under the auspices of providing security for the family, extends to working 12-hour days, bringing work home, and working weekends - perhaps even on holidays.

And when conflict arises in the home because of this work ethic, the justification is usually the same: "I'm doing this for the family."

Of course, part of this justification is valid.

However, the more profound truth lies in the meaning given to an excessive work ethic, which is fear.

It is the fear of losing one's job, losing a client, being left behind for promotions, not being seen as committed, and an unwillingness to create an individualised way of working - to be your own woman or man.

By asking the question, what meaning does a particular activity/behaviour/belief/emotion give your life? You formulate a reasoned insight into whether the meaning feeds fear, ego or something else, regardless of any justification or elements of denial one might offer.

After all, one can safely assess what meaning a person has given to aspects of their life if, for example, they engage in:

- Conflict
- Sexism
- Racism
- Bullying
- Arrogance
- Vanity
- Fear of missing out
- Conflict avoidance
- Blame
- Unassertiveness
- Jealousy
- Materialism
- Paranoia
- Petulance

Of course, the converse is also true, but whatever you decide is essential in your life and gives you meaning remains a choice only you can make.

Living the Two Truths requires a choice between the negative and positive, fact over fiction, and the meaningful over the irrelevant and damaging.

May your choices reflect your hopes not your fears.

Viktor Frankl, the eminent psychiatrist, author, and Holocaust survivor, knew profoundly that choice in life was critical. He said, *"Everything can be taken from a man but one thing: the last of the human freedoms—to choose one's attitude in any given set of circumstances, to choose one's own way."*

For example, by choosing (*one's own way*) to be unassertive and submissive, your life has a different quality and meaning compared to being assertive and forthright. In either condition, we choose to enjoy or endure the associated consequences.

Or, to use the biblical maxim, you reap what you sow.

There are, of course, many contributing external factors that may influence choosing one's own way. The critical word here is *'influence'*. These external influencing factors are facets of perception and perspective.

Perception is the process of interpreting sensory information, while perspective is the overall framework through which we view the world. Perception is immediate and sensory-based, while perspective is a broader, more abstract concept encompassing our beliefs and values.

For example, Alexi Navalny, the Russian opposition leader, lawyer and anti-corruption activist, endured a murder attempt, torture, and imprisonment and ultimately died in a Russian Gulag in Siberia.

His later life was likely peppered with anxiety and fear regarding the Russian government's attempts to discredit and remove him from the international and domestic arena - his **_perception_**.

However, his **_perspective_** was clear. The Russian people were being lied to, suppressed, and brainwashed by a ruthless and psychopathic leader.

Despite knowing the likely outcome of his open opposition to Putin and his acolytes, Alexi Navalny chose his way. He gave his life meaning.

Not all of us are called upon to stand courageously against a despot. However, we may be called upon to stand against a bullying boss or act as a whistleblower in a corrupt institution, leave an abusive relationship, say no to a friend's request, lose toxic friends, and leave a disempowering job.

In all the above life situations and the many more that could be cited, one's thoughts when deciding to make a major decision will be drawn, understandably, to negative perceptions associated with fear and loss.

However, one's perspective that you deserve only the very best in your life can outweigh negative perceptions by not using the shifting sands of emotions to make decisions to better your life, but the cold hard logic of the question, "What one decision will make me happier and help me move forward in my life?"

As humans with free agency, choice is an intrinsic part of life that carries a fundamental maxim we must accept. Whatever our choices in life, we must take 100% accountability for them by standing in our truth.

Personal perceptions may or may not influence your choices, but whether you bend to those perceptions remains 100% your choice. In everyday life, when fully employed, this maxim means there is no room for shifting blame, assuming the role of a victim, or decrying your circumstances.

Of course, it is a challenging maxim to embrace, but it has benefits. It forms a firm foundation for learning and emotionally growing by exciting new levels of self-empowerment. It offers someone who takes 100% accountability for their choices a mechanism for understanding that their potential is limited only by their perceptions, perspectives and choices.

Therefore, if we accept that happiness is a desired and preferred state, we can also accept that what stands in the way of joy are choices fuelled by fear or ego.

As previously described, fear is a state conjured by the mind to suggest you will lose something treasured - money, status, power, career, love, etc.

Throughout history, great women and men on the national and international stage have made difficult choices despite what appeared to be overwhelming perceptions of the consequences of their beliefs and actions.

Equally, millions of unreported and courageous choices are currently made in families, workplaces, communities and individual lives. When you review their lives, you will see that they all have three traits that support them in making difficult choices. Those traits are:

- They ground and regulate any fear in reality, objectivity and logic. *They mastered fear by abiding in the present.*
- They understood their self-worth and were unencumbered by wanting or needing the approbation of others. *They mastered their ego.*
- They embraced the idea that some choices may cause personal loss, allowing them to move forward without regret. *They mastered detachment.*

These three traits - fear mastery, ego detachment, and self-worth understanding - are not just tools for making difficult choices. They are the keys to self-empowerment, which means having and taking control over our lives.

TAKING CONTROL

It is said that the mind seeks harmony. In doing so, the mind works hard against fear and ego to help us gain control and work towards whatever will make us happy.

However, by accepting that control is not absolute concerning other people, nature, and the future, we realise that many things we generate anxiety over are futile.

In everyday life, our thoughts, feelings, and behaviours are within our control - no matter how difficult and tiring it can sometimes be to exercise that control.

Understanding the three types of control and their distinctions clarifies the differences between what we can and cannot control and empowers us.

When we grasp these distinctions, the maxim about taking 100% accountability for our lives, and how it relates to and combines with control and choice, we become less attached and more empowered, putting ourselves in the driver's seat of our own lives.

Direct control: Everything we feel and think and our responses (behaviour) in any circumstance or situation.

Indirect control: Interactions with others or groups of people who possess control factors that may positively or negatively influence our desired outcomes.

No Control: Extraneous factors determined by natural laws, such as Mother Nature, death, and the future.

One may argue that control is merely a feature of choice driven by our need for internal harmony. After all, if you are attached to an outcome, you seek some form of control.

Control events before they control you.

In Zen philosophy, there is a belief that attachment is the source of all suffering. This statement makes perfect sense when you consider that when you don't get something you want (attachment), you feel disappointed (suffering).

Consequently, there is a direct correlation between the levels of control we demand and exert upon an outcome and the level of disappointment we feel when it doesn't happen.

Ultimately, personal control and 100% accountability are not just concepts, but reflections of our choices. They are reflected in our choices about thinking, feeling, and behaving. This understanding places the power in our hands, reminding us that we are the architects of our lives.

We can choose to heap unhappiness upon ourselves as we try to control the uncontrollable, or we can choose a different path.

We can generate a heart-centred acceptance that brings relief and inner peace, allowing us to navigate life's uncertainties with a calm and steady mind.

And this inner peace sits at the centre of the Two Truths.

CHAPTER 3
Learn To Love

There is no need to learn about love. After all, what is there to know? One simply feels it - right?

Regrettably, when we observe the numerous conflicts that plague our world, it becomes evident that love and its associated qualities: kindness, compromise, compassion, forgiveness, and respect- are not practised or as widespread as they should be.

Love, a profoundly biological and intrinsically spiritual force, is not confined to a select few.

It permeates every aspect of our lives if we choose to embrace it. It belongs to and is part of our humanity that is marrow deep and has been a constant companion since the dawn of time.

Indigenous American cultures link love of self and others to the four-chambered heart, with the heart seen as the bridge between Father Heaven and Mother Earth.

Each chamber of the heart represents a crucial aspect of a heart-centric life, akin to the different rooms in a house, each with its unique purpose:

- **Full-hearted** - to be passionate and live your life with vigour, gratitude, forgiveness and variety.
- **Open-hearted** - to be kind, honest, and generous.
- **Clear-hearted** - to have a clear understanding and belief of your direction in life, your level of self-worth and your innate gifts and abilities.
- **Strong-hearted** - to display courage, willpower, and resilience in the face of difficulty or suffering.

If we honestly ask ourselves, "What is the condition of my four-chambered heart?" we may discover that a facet of our life is out of sync or missing.

The heart plays the most significant role throughout our lives. It is the central player in choosing a partner, embracing a life purpose, engaging in a creative endeavour, learning something new, and, of course, grieving.

Without its influence, we cannot heal trauma, soften a stubborn heart, show compassion, exercise forgiveness or successfully manage fear and ego.

We know that a 'broken heart' or a failed relationship can have disastrous effects. Bereavement disrupts homeostasis and has been known to precipitate death. The mind-body connection is never more acute than when love or its absence is involved.

When loving relationships are absent, humankind fails to flourish, even if its other basic needs are met.

However, the transformative power of social interactions, which trigger cognitive and physiological processes that influence emotional and mental states, can bring about positive change - a fact the world discovered during and after the COVID crisis.

Conversely, heart-based stress, such as grief, loneliness, loss, or fear, is an epigenetic phenomenon that is strongly associated with bodily inflammation and disease.

In essence, what one thinks and feels is translated into biological chemistry that determines one's levels of biological wellness.

And so, an absence of love can trigger feelings of loneliness, pessimism, detachment, insularity, resentment and depression. In response to this isolation, stress hormones are released, which attacks the immune system.

There are plenty of published academic research papers that report how isolation, loneliness and an absence of social connectivity increase the risk (30%-60%) of cardio-health disease (CHD).

It is estimated that 7% of the UK's population (over 3 million) suffers from chronic loneliness (meaning they feel lonely often or always).

This underscores the importance of not just being around people but fostering meaningful social connections.

Even the ancient writer of Proverbs knew something about the heart when he wrote, "*Keep thy heart with all diligence; for out of it are the issues of life.*"

In 1624, John Donne penned:

'*No man is an island,*
Entire of itself,
Every man is a piece of the continent,
A part of the main.'
One might suggest that love, too, is not an island when it comes to ourselves and others.

The need to connect to others to experience different aspects of love is evident. With that connection, important social emotions that form aspects of love are generated - emotions and behaviours like kindness, service, support, sacrifice and empathy.

As essential as connecting to others is, so is the need to connect to ourselves and nourish self-love.

SELF LOVE

If self-love can be defined as an appreciation of one's worth, then we must recognise that too much or insufficient self-love may negatively influence our psyches.

Healthy self-love rests in a balanced state at the centre of two polar extremes: narcissism and low self-esteem. And the journey to either of the extremes starts in the centre - healthy self-love.

I say journey because one does not go to sleep enjoying a healthy state of self-love and then awake in the morning as a narcissist or someone filled with self-loathing.

The journey is full of complex emotional and cognitive deliberations, fuelled by a single or a series of circumstances that change established belief systems and behaviours.

And whichever end of the scale one finds themselves, there is a price to pay.

When self-love is absent, we have difficulty believing in ourselves. We spend a lot of time comparing ourselves with others, discounting our competency, devaluing our contributions, disparaging our looks, dismissing achievements and judging ourselves too harshly.

When self-love is overstated, and the ego is free to write and believe its distorted press releases, you see a glut of arrogance, pride, boasting, intellectual dogma, selfishness and a disconnection from reality.

Self-love is not a passive feature of the human psyche, and so it needs conscious effort to develop and embed it so that it is not shaken by self-doubt, or the doubt imposed by others.

There are five essential ways to develop self-love.

Self-knowledge - As Aristotle wisely posits, *'Knowing yourself is the beginning of wisdom.'* But what exactly is this 'self' that we are urged to know?

Is it the personality we need to have greater knowledge of, or is it a more profound developmental construct?

The Hellenic concept of eudaimonia believes that self-knowledge involves knowing and living by the truth in one's spirit or daemon.

This understanding of self-knowledge transcends the personality to encompass the inner soul or, in modern parlance - the higher self or psyche.

True self-love is having knowledge and understanding of the inner you.

As Narcissus tragically demonstrates, selfishness and self-obsession result from searching for one's identity externally. He gained his superficial sense of self from the false perception he gained from his reflection.

Therefore, we must carefully and lovingly question our self-perceptions, which we have chosen as defence mechanisms, walls of solitude, learned but unhelpful behaviours and attitudes, and features of social norm and compliance.

Questioning delusions is the first step in undoing them.

Often, our self-perceptions are delusional, and to develop self-knowledge, we must learn to question why we think, feel and behave in a certain way.

Employing the aphorism, *'It's not my fault, it's just the way I am,'* is an excellent example of a shallow and lazy acceptance by someone who avoids meaningful self-reflection and the associated work to develop.

The first step in gaining true self-knowledge is reconnecting to the real you, and a helpful approach to do this might be to ask questions like:

- What reasons are there that I people please so much?
- What is the trigger for me losing my temper so readily?
- How do I break the habit of always sacrificing my needs for others?
- What is the root of my feeling that I am a victim?
- Why am I so defensive?
- What is it that I don't do that by doing will make me happier and more fulfilled?

The list, as you might imagine, is endless.

Of course, it is reasonable to view your psyche and consider that you may have outgrown or, in some cases, dislike specific characteristics of your humanness.

However, you mustn't apportion a negative judgment to those realisations because this might lead to a spiraling sense of self-worth. Your observations are a call to action - nothing more.

Review what aspects you no longer need and consider them with an enquiring and learning mind, not a mind intent on reprimanding yourself for not being better, stronger or more self-empowering.

Such self-assessments are futile and a very subjective exercise. Self-knowledge is the jewel of all knowledge because it connects us to others in a more heart-centric way.

We begin to understand that limiting and disempowering how we interact with the world deprives others of our very best selves.

By being aloof, we disconnect. By being angry, we rob ourselves and others of peace. By being self-centred, we fail to be compassionate. By being scared, we fail to stand up for what is right.

And by being arrogant, we lose the ability to be trusted. The theme of connection and all the features of self-love will be recurring.

The ancient philosopher Hierocles offered sound advice when he said, "Act by everyone, in the same manner as if you supposed yourself to be him, and him to be you."

A *do unto others as they would do unto you* maxim is a perfect place to start self-knowledge.

In other words, what's the impact of me doing or not doing certain things on others? After all, don't you want the best for you and so, why not the best for others too?

Personal accountability - The root of authenticity is individual accountability.

One might possess self-knowledge about a specific attitude, belief or behaviour but choose not to take accountability for its impact on yourself and others.

When ditching personal responsibility, people tend to:

- Blame others for it being part of their psyche
- Blame circumstances and stress
- Rationalise or dilute the real impact of the trait
- Embrace the trait and embed it as a part of their identity, no matter the impact

Let's take the example of a jealous boyfriend. His jealousy converts into controlling behaviour, inner rage, and blame towards his partner. Again, we see fear and ego in play.

Daily comments arise such as, "You make me feel jealous - It's your fault I act the way I do because you won't let me check your phone - It's not you I don't trust, it's the people you hang about with socially," become the standard way he conducts himself in the relationship.

His failure to take full accountability for his jealousy is holding back his emotional development, impacting his self-esteem and slowly destroying the relationship.

Although jealousy has been used as an example, I might have highlighted traits such as selfishness, fear, anger, lying, committing crimes, pessimism, laziness, etc.

And because humankind has free agency to choose its way, many people take 100% accountability for everything in their lives and move forward in achieving their goals.

This choice - this commitment to personal growth and improvement, holds the potential to transform lives. Of course, many do not.

Although this is their prerogative, they forgo the right to look externally for reasons they have yet to get what they want.

In life and all our cases, the idiom *'The buck stops here'* applies.

In his doctrine on virtue, Aristotle argued that true lovers of themselves display a love for rational planning that results in activities that express themselves and their potentialities.

This virtue is the aspect of self-love that encourages us to engage in endeavours which are meaningful and pleasing to ourselves.

It is a self-navigating mechanism that avoids the need for social approval and enjoys being original, creative, self-actualising and resilient.

What we decide to do is our unique contribution to the world. At its purest, self-accountability is a form of service to humankind. It provides a way of making what we do matter authentically.

It allows us to be accountable for how we grow and how that growth may support and make a difference to others. When we fail to take accountability, our self-love is disrupted.

This lack of accountability is because we nurture victimhood, blame others and our circumstances, and rationalise why we are developmentally inert.

Consequently, self-love becomes fractured because self-esteem is associated with having a sense of purpose - a direction and achieving or working towards goals, no matter how small.

Equally, it is important to avoid becoming overly zealous about setting and achieving goals. Confucius highlighted this precept by saying, "*Roads were made for journeys, not destinations.*"

Determining your desired journey requires aligning your heart with purposeful and motivating things.

For example, undertaking a job role in which your heart is not fully committed can lead to unhappiness, poor health, and stress.

Too many people spend their lives around activities to which they have no deep commitment other than as a source of money, relationship security, political gain, bragging rights, hopes of gaining favour or superficial entertainment.

Of course, money has its place. However, the consequences of making money, your job, your reputation, your likeability, the sole interest in your life - your God, one might say- will cost relationships, well-being, and integrity.

Worse still, a prolonged pursuit of what empties your heart will one day cause you to experience a profound longing to bring real meaning to your life and then be too fearful to do so.

The DNA of personal accountability is bringing meaning to one's life and to have one's life have meaning.

As we do this, we must remember that, like anything related to self-love, we must walk the accountability journey, accepting that we will likely make some errors - and that's perfectly okay.

After all, forgiving yourself is also a part of taking personal accountability.

Self-healing - In a world where big Pharma has predominated for decades, the first challenges to its dominance and efficacy come from different and surprising alternatives.

These alternatives range from the ancient world of meditation to clinical studies involving the use and benefit of psilocybin in treating mental health conditions and the use of energy healing in hospices.

The mind-body connection is no longer on the fringes of mainstream clinical understanding; it is at the forefront of a growing appreciation that healing does not have to come from a bottle or syringe.

Eminent scientists and researchers are reinforcing this fact.

In her book Molecules of Emotion: The Science Behind Mind-Body Medicine, Dr. Candace Pert famously said, "When emotions are expressed...all systems are united and made whole. When emotions are repressed, denied, or not allowed to be whatever they may be, our network pathways get blocked, stopping the flow of the vital feel-good, unifying chemicals that run both our biology and our behaviour."

Dr. Bruce Lipton, a highly renowned and respected cell biologist, has stated that *stress - in its many forms, is the cause of at least 95% of all* illness and disease.

But what does self-healing have to do with self-love?

If we accept that much of our lives revolve around our work, we can also assume that work may impact our health and well-being and we may not be aware its happening.

Some eye-watering statistics from the business intelligence and data insight company Statista and the online community YouGov UK support this premise.

Statista found that 79% of people report that work-related stress is the most common cause of illness. Additionally, they report that inpatient hospital admissions caused by stress-related illnesses in the UK cost around £8.13bn.

Meanwhile, YouGov UK discovered that 46% of respondents say that they eat too much or too unhealthily due to stress and that 29% say that due to stress, they started drinking or increased their drinking.

Of course, these and other comparable statistics are widely known and reported.

One might reasonably infer from this data that people invest too heavily in their professional lives while forgoing essential aspects of their health.

Skipping or rushing lunches, taking work home, using mobile technology for work-related issues during leisure time, and enduring toxic relationships at work all negatively impact our hearts, minds, cellular health, and psyche.

If unregulated and unmanaged, work stressors can significantly impact an individual's well-being, and a family's harmonious cohesion and well-being.

Self-healing aims to mitigate any negative stress on the body and spirit. Stress, wherever it originates, generates trauma that is absorbed. This trauma can come from various circumstances but will predominantly come from what we think and feel.

Trauma can also include environmental factors such as the food and drink we ingest, electronic devices, noise, and other people's negative energy.

When it comes to trauma, stress and inflammation, the body keeps score, and it tries to get your attention by signposting an underlying problem.

So, whenever you feel a little off, lack energy, experience insomnia, lack appetite, or have recurring bouts of sickness, your body is not just telling you to pay attention; it's asking you to listen and take action.

In modern terms, if we have a headache, we take a pill; if we can't sleep, we take a pill, and if we are stressed, we resort to denial or avoidance until our mind and body break down.

This cycle happens because the mind-body connection, a powerful force, can be both a source of good and bad for our health.

For example, it is no casual coincidence that stress causes inflammation of:

The heart (*taking things to heart* - coronary disease, high blood pressure)

The mind (*not thinking straight* - depression, insomnia, migraine)

The gut (*sick to the stomach* - IBS, autoimmune diseases, prostate disease)

Additionally, many studies link inflammation in its many guises, including stress-driven inflammation, to various cancers.

Consequently, it is critical to our overall wellness that we find and take time to self-heal - to recuperate and restore what has been traumatised to health.

And the marvellous thing about the body is that it will often perform miracles given time and the proper healing modality.

Taking time to heal our body, mind, and spirit is an essential act of self-love and is a working confirmation that we matter.

Self-acceptance—Since the dawn of humanity, two questions, above all others, have infiltrated humanity's psyche: "Who am I, and what is my purpose?"

Or as Mark Twain asserted - the *two* most important days in your life are the day you are born and the day you find out why

At the core of these questions is a desire to know the real you—your true identity and purpose. The problem that often arises in undertaking this lifelong quest is that we don't always approach self-acceptance in a balanced way.

We dwell on what we dislike about ourselves and usually dilute, dismiss, or deny our positive qualities. This biased self-judgement leads to various complications, the foremost of which is low self-esteem.

We forget that external factors influence how we see ourselves from birth to our formative years. Friends, family, society, religion, and culture are just a few of the environmental norms that can wreak havoc on our self-worth and self-belief.

Learning to love is the first of our Two Truths, and self-acceptance is critical to living them.

We must understand that the complexity of our lives is part of what it is to be human. The fact that we hold ourselves against a particular standard, despite the complexity, points towards our inner nobility and desire to learn and improve.

Problems arise when the self-critic dominates. Self-criticism is unbalanced, subjective and disempowering.

It has no regard for your well-being or desire to move you forward. The yin and yang of self-acceptance is illustrated in the following Native American story, as an old Cherokee Indian chief teaches his grandson about life.

"A fight is going on inside me," he told the young boy, "A fight between two wolves.

The Dark one is evil - he is anger, envy, sorrow, regret, greed, arrogance, self-pity, guilt, resentment, inferiority, lies, fear, superiority, and ego.

The Light Wolf is good - he is joy, peace, love, hope, serenity, humility, kindness, benevolence, empathy, generosity, truth, compassion, and faith.

The same fight is going on inside you grandson and inside of every other person on the face of this Earth."

The grandson ponders this for a moment and then asked, "Grandfather, w*hich wolf will win?*"

The grandfather smiled and said, "*The one I feed*".

If we can accept that we only want the best for ourselves, then dwelling on what we believe to be our character flaws is in direct opposition to that goal.

Nobility is within all of us and is exemplified by the many acts of kindness, sacrifice, philanthropy, love, and support worldwide - everyday clues to our divine origin - not our biological makeup.

I firmly believe that the foundation of self-acceptance is the knowledge that we are of divine origin.

Beyond the narrow constructs offered by religion, science, and evolution is the gnawing knowledge that we belong to something more profound than the biological conglomeration known as our body.

And if one can accept the premise that we are more, more of what?

Emily Dickinson once wrote:

This World is not Conclusion.
A Species stands beyond -
Invisible, as Music -
But positive, as Sound -
It beckons, and it baffles -
Philosophy, dont know -
And through a Riddle, at the last -
Sagacity, must go -
To guess it, puzzles scholars -
To gain it, Men have borne
Contempt of Generations
And Crucifixion, shown -
Faith slips - and laughs, and rallies -
Blushes, if any see -
Plucks at a twig of Evidence -
And asks a Vane, the way -
Much Gesture, from the Pulpit -
Strong Hallelujahs roll -
Narcotics cannot still the Tooth
That nibbles at the soul -

In her poem, Emily Dickinson refers to an unseen knowing that nibbles at the soul. Many well-known luminaries have felt this same knowing and accepted the idea of an immortal existence.

For example, Srinivasa Ramanujan was a self-taught Indian mathematician who attended Cambridge University and became a Fellow of The Royal Society.

He is known for his incredible mathematical insights and contributions to number theory, infinite series, and continued fractions.

However, one of the most insightful details of Ramanujan's work is his claim that he discovered many of his mathematical insights by communicating with Namagiri, the Hindu Goddess of creativity.

This renowned logician openly admitted he had help from the metaphysical - the spiritual realm.

And he is not the only one. Thomas Edison, Arthur Conan Doyle, Gustav Jung, Galileo, Marie Curie, and Albert Einstein, to name just a few, also believed strongly in the idea of a soul.

I realise this notion of combining immortality and humanity is an antithesis of the agnostic and atheist.

Such ideas are pie in the sky for those who seek absolute proof before a concrete pronouncement can be made about life after death or our divine origins.

However, let's embark on the journey of self-discovery and embrace our true identity and worth. By so doing, we open ourselves to a world of knowledge about ourselves, others, and the vast universe we inhabit.
We realise that we are a work in progress, a beautiful and evolving entity, regardless of the opinions of social influencers, critics, or our self-judgements. A perfect imperfection.

Equally, it is normal and acceptable to recognise that we lack specific knowledge, understanding and proficiency in life. But this understanding stands on the shoulders of an objective evaluation, not a self-demeaning assassination of self.

We must learn to compassionately accept who we are and avoid seeking acceptance from those who wish to tell us, based on their limited understanding, what and who we are or should be.

Self-acceptance will make you less afraid of life and, in particular, the judgements of others. This acceptance allows us to pursue our interests and passions, despite naysayers, and life's various obstacles.

Self-acceptance also means understanding the futility of pursuing a risk-free existence that either keeps you in your comfort zone or overextends one's need to get things right -always. The root of this folly is wanting to be perfect or safe.

Perfectionism is an illusion. There is always room for growth, improvement, and new ways of viewing the world.

Suppose your desire to be perfect is motivated by wanting to impress or appease others, be safe or avoid failure. If so, you can expect to enjoy your fair level of associated anxiety, stress, illness and fear. As I say, it is a folly.

Self-acceptance is an essential discipline for daily life. By accepting that we are on a journey, it is inevitable that mistakes will happen, and lessons will be learnt. This acceptance allows the human experience to become less tense, anxious, and fraught with a desire to be perfect and safe.

Perhaps we should take a lesson from the Japanese word and philosophy of '***Wabi Sabi***.'

In traditional Japanese culture, Wabi-sabi is a worldview centred on aesthetics. It appreciates the world's imperfect, impermanent, and incomplete beauty in all its forms.

Wabi-sabi is more than a concept for teacups, sitting rooms, gardens and lawns. It's a universal principle that applies to all aspects of life.

The crack in a teacup, the leaves on a lawn, the skin blemish, the old scar, the wrinkles, the quirky dress sense, the unusual hobby, the missing limb - all are features of wabi-sabi, adding to - not detracting from, the beauty of our world and all in it.

And doesn't wabi-sabi perfectly describe the mortal condition? It is a state of transience and imperfection in which beauty can be found everywhere—especially inside us.

By embracing the first truth - learning to love - we must learn to fully embrace and appreciate our inner beauty and that of others.

Everything external will fade as it faces the march of time, but the beauty inside is eternal and the only unchanging thing about us, and we should embrace it unconditionally.

Transcendence - When living the first truth of learning to love, it can be challenging to move beyond self-focused consciousness and see things as they truly are.

To do this, we must exercise considerable freedom from our social conditioning.

This social conditioning occurs at a conscious and subconscious level as we navigate and fit into the social norms we are exposed to and, to some degree, expected to conform to by parents, friends, the workplace, religion, our culture and society.

The problem with conditioning is that we can disempower ourselves by limiting ourselves to what is expected from others or what we believe we are capable of. Over time, this conditioning converts into delimiting belief systems, which turns into habits and norms.

Our mindset turns into phrases such as 'I can't', 'I'd better not', 'I'll fail', 'What if I'm not perfect?', 'What will others think?' and—my personal favourite - '*I'm not good enough*'.

I mentioned earlier that the fragile ego works hard to protect a position of safety by avoiding challenge and exposure to the truth and protecting itself from failure and shame.

The unfortunate by-product of a fragile ego is that it prevents us from connecting authentically with others. We disconnect from others by default because showing vulnerability is risky, and staying in the shadows is the safest place.

Equally, the ego can drag us into a complex matrix of defence mechanisms that use power plays, vain boasts, extreme moods and varying degrees of entitlement to shore up its fragile position.

However, a balanced and regulated ego loves self and others as its central premise. The healthy ego is comfortable with compromise, forgiveness, honest feedback, vulnerability, self-confidence, apologising, and compassion.

When the ego is transcended, peace follows, and fear disappears. In such moments, you realise what a useless, disempowering and destructive feature of self, the fragile ego, is.

If others use us despitefully, we must endeavour to detach from our ego by overcoming painful feelings that might include powerful emotions like revenge and retribution.

Dwelling on what has been done to us anchors us to the past, destroys our inner peace and fails to help the trauma heal.

While turning the other cheek may seem challenging, it's a philosophy that demands the best of us. It's about detaching from ego, fear, pain and hurt and embracing a higher form of love.

This love can transform us, by removing any barriers hindering our personal growth and connection to others. The African concept of **Ubuntu** (*humanity to others*) - encapsulates this philosophy by reminding us that 'I am what I am because of who we all are.'

Finding human beauty and worth beyond skin colour, economic or employment status, ethnicity, belief systems, and life circumstances is transcendent love.

Transcending their egos, people like Gandhi, Unita Blackwell, Mother Teresa, Nelson Mandela and many others knew the need to exemplify this love by understanding it meant nothing if it wasn't used for the benefit of others.

By transcending the ego and dismissing fear, we would all love ourselves and others unconditionally.

The direct consequence of this happy position is that we would see poverty eliminated, wars cease, racism abhorred, borders fall, well-being improved, the Earth healed, religious contention disappear, homelessness eradicated, and animals respected and loved.

Then, we would finally understand at our very core that everyone and everything on the planet is inextricably connected.

You may think, "Nah... life is not that simple." Or your brain may churn away and conclude: Steve, you are an idealist, dreamer, or just plumb naïve. Perhaps even all three!

Still, before you send me to the 'Get Real' boot camp for ideological reprogramming, I want to offer some pragmatic and considered rationale for adopting Truth #1 - Learn to Love, at a cellular level.

Love sits at the core of who we are as humans. As a species, love is as integral to our survival as our beating heart.

When we take our first breath, we breathe love into our life. And there it sits, waiting for us to nurture and employ it in every aspect of our lives.

Love is demonstrated in our interactions with others and in our jobs, hobbies, food preparation, health, and treatment of Mother Earth.

When someone shows compassion to another, that form of love is unconditional. And, as we know, love is at the core of every selfless act – even the smallest.

A smile, a random act of kindness, opening a door, a compliment, giving money or time to charity, and even a thank you - are features of love.

If we are to learn to love unconditionally, we must be open to inner growth. And the internal growth and change I am talking about comes at a cost.

Put simply, we must lose something to win something - we must lose our fragile ego and fear.

Fear and the negative features of the human ego nurture an absence of love and promote a platform of exclusion and disconnection. It is a disconnection from nature, the environment, animals, the planet, and each other - especially those in need.

The greater an individual, community, or society's disconnection from love, the more significant the impact.

You see examples of fear and the insular ego at work in destructive belief systems and behaviours that nourish:

Nuclear proliferation	Misogyny
Destroying the rainforest	Terrorism
Religious intolerance	Political self-interest
Homophobia	Corporate self-interest
Climate change	Genocide
Cruelty towards animals	Civil wars
Racism	Despotic rule
Financial avarice	Online Trolling

Central to our humanistic values is the understanding that we are all connected. It is a 'whatever you do to another, you do it to me too' philosophy.

Learning to love becomes much easier when we suppress our ego and encourage the schooling, regulation, refinement and development of our emotions and belief systems.

We all seek human connection and love is the word we use for that search.

We need more agape love in the world. Agape love is selfless—it is love for humanity. It is the closest to unconditional love, and it is love that you give expecting nothing in return.

When you seek out instances of agape love, you'll find them. In those moments when someone makes a personal sacrifice, no matter how small, you witness agape love.

Each act of love and kindness deepens our humanity and gives us a sense of purpose in connecting with others.

By performing a kindness, you are embracing agape love. Agape love, encapsulated in Truth #1, is a perpetual, ever-evolving, always-improving, never-too-big, never-too-small, never-too-late, forever-blooming way of life.

It's a belief I hold dear that we all yearn for human connection, and 'love' is the term we use to express that longing.

The Indian mystical poet Kabir beautifully phrased this idea when he said, "The river that flows in you also flows in me."

He proposes that if you think of hurting another or yourself, you might ask this simple question: "What would 'love' do in this situation?"

Love is the antithesis of anything negative, demeaning, degrading, selfish, apathetic or conflict-orientated. And so, if you discover that your ego or perhaps an aspect of fear in your life is stopping you from nurturing and practising love, I urge you to work hard to remove that element.

Equally, do not accept as fact anyone telling you we live in a loveless world or that love doesn't change a thing.

These unworthy sentiments do not reflect the truth, regardless of the justification for such a jaded view of love and humankind.

We need to recognise that for every act of evil and meanness in the world, there is a counterbalance that sees those acts outweighed by countless examples of love, kindness, generosity and acts of service.

So, wherever you find revenge, you will discover forgiveness. Whenever you see hatred, love will be waiting in the wings, and if pride and arrogance cross your path, reassure yourself that humility will soon follow.

However, of all the lies about love, do not tell yourself, not even in the darkest moments, that you are not worthy of love.

The simple truth is that you are love. At your core, you are the embodiment of love, and I hope you learn not only to embrace that eternal truth but also to nurture it, share it, and make it blossom.

CHAPTER 4
Love To Learn

From birth, we've been assimilating knowledge. At every step of life, we embrace information, make sense of it, and hopefully apply it successfully.

We know this process of knowledge assimilation and application as learning. And as many of us know, there can be an enormous gap between knowing something and learning something.

One of our challenges as humans is that we can be the smartest of souls and the dumbest of creatures.

To illustrate this point, one would have thought by now we'd learnt that war solves nothing, that our planet is not a cesspool for waste, that animals have feelings, and that nobody in society should go hungry, be homeless, or feel victimised for the colour of their skin or their gender.

I know… I know… the dreamer has resurfaced!

*Forever learning but never coming to the knowledge of
the truth*

But in my defence, I've yet to meet a single, sober, rational-minded person who disagrees with my premise that sometimes, we don't learn from our mistakes.

That said, each of the lovely folk who are kind enough to listen to me, challenge my idealism or offer the well-meant dismissal of, "Well, the problem is just too big: what can I do? After all, I'm just one person?"

My sense is that there is plenty we can do. Helen Keller, once said, *"I long to accomplish a great and noble task; but it is my chief duty to accomplish small tasks as if they were great and noble."*

We can recycle, vote, lobby our MP, join a pressure group, attend a march, or challenge people who promote antisocial behaviour or misinformation.

Each is a tiny endeavour, but standing in the grey and moaning that nothing changes without doing something to make a change is, at best, unproductive and, at worst, feeding the status quo.

By learning to step outside our Circle of Concern, we free ourselves from worrying about what we can't do or what we don't have. Instead, we focus on what we can do and what we do have, empowering ourselves to make a difference.

The true power of learning lies in its transformative nature. Through our endeavours in learning, we acquire new knowledge and develop our character.

Learning is a journey that empowers us with new perspectives on risk, cultivates courage and resilience, and unlocks our potential, making us more confident in our abilities.

Loving to learn requires self-awareness, and that cannot happen without humility. We must embrace the idea of curiosity by being open to the knowledge, insights, perspectives, and feedback that will help us develop.

Even those we may disagree with.

We do this with an open and objective heart to foster self-acceptance and avoid the trap of self-judgments that can impact our self-regard. This self-acceptance is crucial because mistakes will likely be made along the way.

These mistakes, such as errors of judgment, skewed perspectives, unhelpful belief systems, detrimental habits, ill-advised relationships, and absent knowledge, are necessary for learning and personal growth.

After all, how can a woman or a man understand what they will be tomorrow if they do not understand the child they are today?

Of course, by choosing to learn about ourselves and the world around us, we foster a more integrated appreciation and compassion for Mother Earth and humanity.

We begin to understand differing perspectives and learn about why we do the things that we do that hurt ourselves and others.

No solution can possibly exist while you are lost in the energy of a problem.

To ensure that loving to learn becomes a way of life, we must recognise that we not only deserve but also have a collective responsibility to grow.

We must develop individually and collectively as a species and understand that living Truth #2 is more profound than gaining knowledge.

It is about fostering a sense of unity and shared growth.

Learning is a form of love. It's a service to humankind, equipping us with the tools to enhance lives, both of others and our own. This understanding underscores the value of education in making a positive impact.

Loving to learn is a form of self-love because you are investing in the one person who can make a difference within your sphere of influence. Working towards your potential is critical because by doing so, you can fully contribute to humanity.

And that journey of contribution and service starts with how we learn and grow. It involves how we perceive the world, challenges the hard-wired belief systems constricting us, and, perhaps most importantly, learning encourages us to liberate ourselves from fear and ego.

You must objectively observe your problems instead of being lost in them.

Progressive personal growth and self-mastery are about transcending the part of you that seeks to be protected, safe, and secure.

It is understanding that the neurotic, self-judging, self-doubting, frightened, distracting voice inside your head does not have your best interests at heart. It wants you to avoid tough emotional and mental challenges and choices.

You will meaningfully grow and empower yourself once you wrestle control from your doubting and critical inner voice and objectively observe your challenges instead of being lost in them.

So, where does a person start? In a word – humility.

Humility requires a lot of emotional effort because the ego has a consistent - some might say constant - motivation to be heard, be correct, and win.

The ego rarely surrenders, and when it does because of fear, people suffer from meekness, low self-esteem, and trauma-related illnesses.

In humility, we find vulnerability; in vulnerability, we discover our true worth and the courage that supports us in being who we are and what we can be.

The ego unharnessed is a marauding wolf with a voracious appetite. It is happy to devour and thrive on an appetite of pride, fear, dogmatism, laziness, pseudo-intellectualism, academic snobbery and ignorance.

The ego is an immense barrier to self-development, especially if our viewpoints are hard-wired, habitual, and non-changing perspectives.

A bad day for your ego is a great day for your soul.

Ernest Hemingway once said, *"There is nothing noble in being superior to your fellow man; true nobility is being superior to your former self."*

Making incremental gains against your former self is a noble pursuit because you endeavour to be less of what you were and more of what you could be.

This approach requires hard questions that, if honestly considered, may reveal uncomfortable answers.

They are questions that will challenge habits, outdated knowledge, hard-wired beliefs, and damaging mindsets. But remember, it's in these challenges that we find our strength and capability to learn and progress.

At a personal level, we might ask ourselves:

- Why am I so defensive?
- Why do I always have to be right?
- What is the difficulty with me saying sorry?
- Why do I *choose* to live in fear?
- Why do I keep feeling so negatively about myself?
- Why am I choosing to hold on to this fear/grudge/bitterness/loss/belief?
- When I behave like this, who am I really hurting?
- What stops me from believing in myself?
- What causes me to be angry - fearful - judgemental - closed - frustrated - insular?
- What is stopping me from gaining more knowledge?
- Is there a reason I won't accept help?
- Why am I so afraid of making a mistake?
- Why do I think my perspectives are more valid?
- Why do I care so much about what others think?

True humility is not in the absence of confidence - but strength restrained.

Emotional attachments to safety and security often restrict personal growth and learning. They deter us from engaging in conflict, resisting change, and making the difficult, yet courageous, choices that are necessary for our development.

It seems incongruent that we live in an age where many political and corporate leaders ***choose*** to ignore lessons that should have been learned decades ago.

By choosing to ignore these lessons, humanity is plagued with:

- Nuclear weapons
- Mass agricultural and animal farming using chemical pesticides
- Polluting the planet
- Delaying environmental initiatives
- War
- Social inequality
- Corporate greed
- Populist politics to retain power

As a noun, choice often denotes the options available between various alternatives. Now, I don't know about you, but when offered choices, I tend to opt for the best one.

Why is it then, I wonder, that a clear choice to stop something so damaging as polluting the planet is diluted into a halfway house built on shifting sands?

There have been countless conferences and summits where a nation's political or corporate leaders were insufficiently strong enough to do the right thing.

Exhibiting a blatant inability to listen and learn from what scientists, the weather, Mother Earth, animals, and common sense have been telling them for decades.

In the same vein, one would have thought that the first nuclear mushroom cloud would have offered sufficient data for us to learn that atomic weapons benefit no one - a lesson we should have gleaned from the quarter of a million innocent Japanese souls who died in that act of nuclear horror and stupidity.

Global leaders too readily use procrastination and appeasement in clearly black-and-white matters, where no grey is required.

At some point, we will collectively challenge the damaging, outdated, and controlling ideologies found in the military, the government, and corporations.

Equally, I hope that we take greater responsibility individually to spotlight our emotional development, harmful belief systems, and disempowering mindsets so that we may move closer to our highest potential.

At its core, learning is a transformative process. It is how we discover the truth and make improvements. Truth does not dwell in the grey or shadows and is not a friend to ego, control, or fear.

Learning is not just a means to an end; it is a vibrant way to enrich our lives, protect the planet, foster love for our neighbours, and secure our children's future.

It is a beacon of progress, guiding us towards a better world. Its value extends beyond personal growth, making it a crucial societal development and well-being aspect.

Embracing the Second Truth offers a beautiful humanistic duality. It allows us to understand and master ourselves, and by so doing, we harmonise our relationship with ourselves, others and the planet.

We can do this by not occupying the narrow-minded state the ego insists is our default position.

The inner state blames others, avoids taking 100% accountability, judges others too quickly, avoids the truth because it is too painful, believes you have learned everything and accepts the lie you can't change because it's *just the way you are*.

This narrow-minded conditioning is the breeding ground for religious zealots, extreme left - or right-wing ideologies, and belief systems that found their first breath centuries ago. It generates barriers to our development as a species by propagating a starting position that insists that our position is correct, valid, and irrefutable.

However, we can learn from all life situations, including adversity. Better still, we can learn from nature, the young, the old, the unexplained, and the whopping big mistakes we've made – even the reoccurring ones.

Let me go further: learning opportunities are everywhere; we need only have a desire to look. And paradoxically, we can also learn from and show gratitude to those who challenge and hurt us most.

After all, these individuals stimulate our development by testing our desire and ability to be patient, forgive, demonstrate empathy, and exercise fortitude and love because of their interventions or lack thereof.

History's great women and men have exemplified this soul-level perspective on rising above our human conditioning. These paragons elevated their humanism to show that it can be done.

They conquered fear and their egos because their self-love demanded something more from them - to access and activate their true - their higher character.

The route to gaining access to our true character starts with asking ourselves some fundamental questions, the principal being, "*Why do I do - what do I do?*"

Honestly answered, this question may uncover fragile traits such as vanity, pride, defensiveness, victimhood, jealousy, social recognition and acceptance, and the need to be right or perfect.

And if you want to embrace the Second Truth of loving to learn, there are other questions you could ask:

- How did I contribute to this situation?
- What are the real reasons I'm feeling this way?
- Why am I holding on to this self-pity?
- Why am I choosing to behave in this way?
- What's the benefit to me by living in the past?
- How is this pain serving me?
- Why am I blaming others for my mistakes?
- How do I make things better?
- What's the lesson for me here?

I acknowledge that these are challenging questions to ask oneself. After all, they demand answers that challenge the ego and belief systems and require us to take personal accountability and growth.

Loving to learn is a heroic endeavour because it requires courage and the acceptance that you might stumble along the way - perhaps even fail a few times. But this is normal in any quest for meaningful personal growth.

Although there can be apprehension about embarking on any learning journey, it must not stop us from starting it. Problems arise when we fear the journey and choose to delay or avoid potentially challenging situations that will help us grow.

One of these self-induced problems is the modern and ill-advised label of *'imposter syndrome'*. The suggestion is that a person settles on the idea that they don't deserve a role or promotion or are not ready.

This mindset exists despite working hard to achieve a step up on the career ladder, being recognised for their progress and being rewarded with the role.

This mindset is not a syndrome but a self-love problem. Once self-love is established and nurtured, there can be no personal doubt or anxiety that what flows to you is deserved.

Failing to live the first truth of learning to love frustrates the second truth of loving to learn. Imagine for a moment what would happen if we truly loved learning about ourselves.

We would take 100% accountability for our lives and ensure that fear never interfered with our goal of developing our potential.

This newfound understanding would encourage us to value others' opinions and embrace the richness of diverse perspectives and approaches. We would discover the power to control our emotions, rewire our subconscious, and shift our thoughts from negativity to positivity.

Most importantly, we would learn to be kinder to ourselves. We would recognise and appreciate that we are all beautiful works in progress and that making mistakes is a natural part of our human journey. Over time, we would let go of harsh self-judgments and unhelpful comparisons that only serve to harm us.

In loving to learn, we need to be more self-compassionate and improve our ability to quash the self-important ego.

Wouldn't it be wonderful if we could laugh at our quirks and stop taking ourselves so seriously? In this way, we would enjoy and be at ease with the idea that mistakes and learning are very close to being members of the same family.

Fear is the gateway to regret.

Fear is one of the most prevalent reasons we shy away from opportunities to learn, grow, and step closer to our beautiful potential. It's a feeling we all know too well.

For example, if you were to ask anyone who, after experiencing a near-death experience (*that's 1 in 8 of us, by the way*), if after visiting the spirit World, they now fear death - to the last one, they would respond with an emphatic no.

Ask the same people if they feared death before their experience, and a considerable percentage will say - most definitely.

The difference between their perspective before and after a near-death experience is their lack of fear. Their fear is replaced with an absolute certainty that life after death unequivocally exists.

And what do these unique folks do after returning from these Near-Death Experiences? They live a life without fear. Go figure!

I appreciate that, at a primordial level, we prefer low-risk environments to satisfy our evolutionary need for physical safety.

And, of course, in our modern age, we are no longer on the menu of sabre-tooth tigers.

This means our need for physical safety has largely been replaced (*courtesy of a bigger brain*) by one of emotional safety.

Herein lies the difference between physical safety and emotional safety. With physical safety, we understandably remove ourselves from danger. However, in protecting ourselves from emotional risk, we tend to prevent ourselves from learning and growing.

If left unchecked, avoiding negative emotions can lead to a various detrimental outcomes. However, by embracing the journey of self-discovery, we open doors to personal growth, insight, and self-mastery.

This perspective shift can ignite feelings of curiosity, empowerment, confidence, and excitement about the potential within us.

Loving to learn is often a challenging journey because it requires us to reevaluate established habits, perceptions, and belief systems. For many, this causes them to feel fearful and vulnerable and to seek emotional safety.

Of course, any learning means emerging from your comfort zone. However, self-growth is not about a '*no pain—no gain*' mindset but about gently embracing a life-long philosophy that loves learning.

And when the time comes to ask for support, do not fear or worry about asking someone for that support. Vulnerability is not a sign of weakness but a sign of trust in another human being and a sign you have overcome the self-protecting ego.

Once we willingly put away our fear and ego, remarkable things happen. We learn with an open heart about ourselves and the world in which we live.

We understand our unique worth and realise we have more control over our thoughts, actions, and emotions than we ever thought possible. And because we enjoy greater awareness and control, we know that whatever we learn will benefit others.

We must adopt a type of learning that goes deep into our psyche, one that sees a passionate pursuit of personal and collective development with love at its core.

For humanity's sake, we must embrace the type of learning that turns the other cheek, walks a mile in the shoes of another, and learns that compromise and alternatives are the hallmarks of a growing soul and species.

For example, it is fascinating to note that those who have embraced metaphysical experiences and expanded their horizons share openly the seeds of such possibilities.

Our era is not just witnessing a revival of ancient esoteric knowledge and practices, but it's being championed by researchers, academics, scientists, and the intellectually and spiritually curious.

In our modern age, we understand only the periphery of what our mind and spirit can achieve.

For example, the medical fraternity discussed the phenomenon known as placebo as early as the 1920s, and in the 1960s, Walter Kennedy added the opposite but associated term of nocebo.

Both terms signpost just one example of the power of the mind, yet powerful and harmful drugs proliferate in medicine. While giant pharmaceutical companies make huge profits, they distract people from the emergence of energy medicine.

To be yourself in a world that is consistently trying to make you something else, is the greatest accomplishment.

Astronauts, pilots, military personnel, and countless civilians report the reality of extraterrestrial beings. Yet cynics and naysayers foster a narrative that suggests these individuals are cranks, liars, easily duped, or just insane.

Consider this: in the vast multiverse, who are you? Are you a mere speck of cosmic dust or an organic being with a future transcending your mortal span? What is your real identity, and how does that inform how you live your life?

Sometimes, pursuing knowledge entails confronting uncomfortable truths about ourselves, the world, and the universe. These truths, though painful, are the bedrock of our understanding and progress.

Of course, in searching for the truth, the ego will apply a fair amount of confirmation bias because challenging established dogma is a problematic premise for many people.

It seems more accessible and safer to nurture a lie and avoid answering a direct question or the effort of pursuing the truth.

It is also easier to hide behind what many people worldwide

consider the arbiters of all truth. Namely, science, academia, religion, or, worse still, a nation's government and its agencies.

After all, we discovered that the Earth is not flat, the world did not take seven days to create, there is more than one galaxy, continental drift exists, the Bible is not chronological and has books missing, and xenotransplantation, or transplanting an animal's organ into a human, is possible.

I would like to encourage you to broaden your horizons, both in terms of knowledge and experience by not being afraid to question what you think you know.

This healthy scepticism is the essence of a love for learning - pursuing truth with an open heart and a curious mind. By doing so, we can grasp our full potential while discarding what might hold us captive to subjective, false and divisive doctrines.

I want to finish this chapter with a Japanese fable about the Scorpion and the Frog.

"A scorpion asks a frog to carry him over a river. The frog is afraid of being stung, but the scorpion argues that if it did so, both would sink, and the scorpion and frog would drown.

The frog then agrees, but midway across the river, the scorpion does indeed sting the frog, dooming them both.

When the frog asks why the scorpion broke his promise, the scorpion says, "I'm sorry. Unfortunately, it is in my nature."

Thankfully, unlike the scorpion, human nature is not immutable - we can flex, adapt and change.

We are born to learn because it blesses us and others. We need not be afraid of Loving to Learn. Neither should it be a burden or a chore. The second of the Two Truths is a way of blessing our lives so that we walk with as little fear and self-doubt as possible.

Inside every living soul is an innate need to reach upwards and progress—to meet the measure of our creation. William Shakespeare hinted that our creation had celestial importance when he said, *"We are a little lower than the angels."*

Imagine if we could catch a glimpse of the realm of the angels. Wouldn't that give us a profound understanding of our true potential and the magnitude of what we can achieve?

It could inspire us to live a life filled with self-appreciation, laughter, creative freedom, forgiveness, and a deep desire to fulfil our life's purpose through learning and growing.

The last words should go to Winnie the Pooh, courtesy of A.A. Milne.

> *You are braver than you believe.*
> *And stronger than you seem.*
> *And smarter than you think.*

CHAPTER 5
One World

To start this chapter, I wish to be contentious. Or at least, disputatious to some.

Atheists and many scientific intellectuals would have us believe that we are nothing more than vehicles of flesh and bone.

They maintain humans do not have a soul, a God being does not exist, life after death is a fantasy, and the idea of an extra-terrestrial species should be left to filmmakers. These tired and rewashed belief systems are always wrapped in the intellectual mantra of *'there is no evidence'*.

Of course, there is evidence, but not their evidence, or at the very least, the type of proof they demand. In many cases, they pursue a confirmation bias that interprets and favours their belief systems, taught by others with similar beliefs.

This cycle of intellectual exploration and growth continues until a new piece of evidence or insight changes their minds because the evidence is worthy of their attention and adoption.

And this is done without the slightest embarrassment about their previous position, but rather, with a motivation to make the new dogma an established truth - until the next time.

I suspect this type of intellectualism offers a dreadful and hopeless death-bed experience as nothingness, as they believe, beckons.

However, I'm delighted that they will not experience nothingness. Such a non-existence flies in the face of the eternal nature of everything about us.

If nature and the cosmos teach us anything, it is the indisputable cycle of birth, death, and rebirth.

Even our Sun, when it dies and becomes a white dwarf star in about 5 billion years, will give life to the far reaches of our solar system and perhaps provide the conditions for the icy realm of Pluto to become habitable.

In their profound wisdom, our ancient ancestors perceived the four seasons not merely as a cycle of nature but as a lived-in metaphor for immortality.

They crafted rituals and ceremonies that mirrored eternal truths, understanding that the cycle of life extended beyond our mortal existence, encompassing the very essence of all living beings, from trees to the animal kingdom.

This spiritual awareness was respected, celebrated, and honoured, informing their healing practices, nomadic habits, and selection of leaders.

That pattern is broken in the modern age. Because of it, we see an epidemic of poor emotional and mental health worldwide, increased conflicts, disconnectedness, and a focus on the material.

Currently, leaders are chosen based on the material wealth of their backers or their inherited wealth, their opportunity for an elite education, or their populist agenda - but never, it seems, for their wisdom or willingness to apologise or admit they are wrong.

To heal as a species and restore balance to our planet, we must look beyond the confines of political, corporate, medical, media, scientific, and religious institutions.

These mainstream entities often perpetuate fear, guilt, control, and despair, hindering collective healing. It is time to seek wisdom from alternative sources - in a more enlightened way.

Moreover, the prevalence of superficial trivia on social media not only distracts but also distorts the minds of the youth. It fosters a culture of accepting falsehoods as truths, compelling them to prioritise superficial lifestyle choices over more meaningful ones.

There are, of course, good people fighting the status quo in strands of society I've mentioned. They are the champions of the impoverished, the misused, the forgotten, the unjustly treated, and the lonely.

They are beacons of goodness who hold the Two Truths at the centre of everything they do.

They are those who fight titans of industry, expose the machinations of politicians, and risk their lives fighting regimes who have weaponised religion to legitimise terrorism, the suppression of women and the wholesale slaughter of ethnic groups.

They are selfless paragons of enlightenment, dedicating themselves to the benefit of others and the planet without the distorted philosophy of profit-making. They are true philanthropists, using their wealth for the betterment of others without seeking recognition or accolades.

They are the uncompromising teachers of truth and the relentless humanitarians who refuse to tolerate ignorance, excuses, or deceit when individuals and groups are in pain.

Sometimes, embodying the Two Truths takes work. It is a way of living that deconstructs the paradigms we've merrily pursued, lived and endured for decades, if not centuries.

The Two Truths are the spiritual scaffolding humanity desperately needs to remove fear, ego and ignorance. They are a clarion call for wholesale change.

The Two Truths are not just principles but a daily practice that reminds us of our true essence - our divine origin. They guide us to understand that we are more than our roles, wealth, or status.

Our divine centre is not a distant concept but an intelligent gateway to our eternal nature, waiting for us to connect and thrive.

Learning to love and ***loving to learn*** is as essential to life as the air we breathe. The Two Truths, when lived, are a joyous thing to our soul and a godsend to those with whom we interact.

The Two Truths embody what it means to be truly human. We see the Two Truths embodied in the daily lives of beautiful souls who perform acts of kindness, sacrifice, charity, and egalitarianism and passionately follow their life's purpose.

They are the uncompromising teachers of truth and the relentless humanitarians who refuse to tolerate ignorance, excuses, or deceit when individuals and groups are in pain.

Living the Two Truths is the genesis of knowledge, insight, creativity, personal challenge, innovation and human development. It is the gentle whispering of wisdom that sits at your core and urges, '*Let the truth set you free*'.

If it is true, as some say, that we live in a cynical world, then this state has developed because too many people have forgotten the Two Truths.

However, as a confessed idealist/optimist whose glass is always half-full (*actually, my optimistic cup regularly overflows*), I'm confident in terms of our development as a species, we are more than equipped to nurture a more enlightened way of loving and learning.

Indeed, let me be bolder and go further. Living the principles embodied in the Two Truths would result in greater human enlightenment, technological advances, social progress, and improved international cooperation and trust.

Additionally, conflicts would decrease, and there could be peace in the world for the first time.

And by enlightenment, I do not mean attaining Nirvana - although that would be nice. I am referring to the personal and collective realisation that we are beings of light, energy, and unlimited potential.

It would change us for the greater good if we embraced the idea that everyone and everything on the planet is connected.

The well-known spiritual tour de force, the Dalai Lama, explained this precept exquisitely when he said:

"Every day, think as you wake up, today I am fortunate to be alive, I have a precious human life, I am not going to waste it. I am going to use all my energies to develop myself, to expand my heart out to others; to achieve enlightenment for the benefit of all beings."

This evolved and loving soul understands the everlasting truth contained in the principles and spiritual philosophies of Two Truths.

In particular, he embraces the expansive philosophy that his life gains a more fulfilling purpose through mindful and inclusive interactions with others.

Like every great spiritual teacher, his message speaks of the need for love in our lives, and we can achieve that by passionately learning from everything and everyone around us.

However, the Two Truths are not reserved only for those we consider enlightened and wise. They are for every soul on Earth. The Two Truths perform the role of a compass in our lives, and like the compass unfailingly pointing to true north, the Two Truths will never mislead you.

Love and learning are not mere concepts; they are potent forces that can elevate us to our higher selves. They pave a path for us as individuals and as a species.

In their beautiful simplicity, they offer a way of life promises happiness, contentment, and peace. Embracing the Two Truths enriches our mortal journey and steers us towards our life's purpose.

This aspect may appear insignificant initially, but in my professional experience, I've encountered numerous (*too many*) individuals who feel they need a sense of purpose.

These individuals reach a point in their lives when they ask themselves deeply reflective questions such as, "*Surely, there has to be more? I should be happy and content, but why do I feel so empty? What is going to make me feel fulfilled?*"

> *True change is within; leave the outside as it is – The Dalai Lama*

We find the answer to these questions by understanding that the Two Truths offer a way to find your life's purpose. We are drawn to our purpose at an early age, and, as any parent will tell you, children live out their life's purpose in the games they play, the books they read, and the activities that absorb them.

But as time progresses, we find that what makes us feel alive and purposeful is derailed. We are sometimes knocked off a purposeful course by the expectations of parents, partners and friends.

Poor career guidance, peer pressure, cultural and societal influences, financial demands, and fear and ego will also play their part.

I have found that when people move further away from a purposeful life, their higher self becomes agitated, dissatisfied, and sad.

Marcus Aurelius understood the reason that a purposeless existence can infiltrate our lives when he wrote, "*If you are distressed by anything external, the pain is not due to the thing itself, but to your estimate of it; and this you have the power to revoke at any moment.*"

For example, suppose you esteem a thing (or an attachment to a thing) highly.

For the purpose of this example, *things* could be money, prestige, health, a job, relationships, or material possessions.

If any of these external things are unexpectedly removed, it may cause you heartache, fear, and pain. In such situations, you have a choice over how much pain you experience and for how long.

Being immersed in these situations is the epitome of attachment and is the core point Marcus Aurelius is making.

A purposeful life based on The Two Truths helps you understand that loving or attaching to transient aspects of life is futile. If we learn to love only those things that truly matter, we will find that fear and unhappiness are uncommon visitors.

Our journey towards a purposeful life involves self-reflection, understanding our ego, and how we interact with and assign power to external elements in our lives.

This awareness offers a great starting point because it helps us identify what aspects of our lives we are enduring because of fear or any negative emotion causing unrest and disharmony.

This mental and emotional unrest can be carried around subconsciously, generating unhelpful and reactive habits that hold us captive to disempowering behaviours and belief systems.

The following allegorical tale beautifully illustrates this concept.

A wise man sat on a stone plinth against the village well and watched the sun rise slowly over the horizon, announcing another day.

Down one of the winding streets that led to the well, a man herding his goats was muttering and cursing under his breath. His face was a canvas of anger, every line etched with irritation and frustration.

"You appear vexed," suggested the wise man.

"I am," said the man. "My neighbour angers me. I hate him and the ground he walks on."

"And yet, the teacher replies, you bring him to work with you."

(From the book: Ten Villages, One Flower: A Wise Man's Journey)

Of all his choices that day, the goatherd embraced enmity towards his neighbour - a product of his ego.

This self-inflicted emotional burden weighed him down as he worked. A stark illustration of the destructive power of ego-driven emotions.

We do not know what caused the goatherd to be so angry.

However, I have seen similar emotional choices and associated behaviours by people nurturing minor sleights, envy, resentments, and immature grudges.

All, without exception, labouring under the illusion that holding onto historical antipathies somehow serves them.

Paradoxically, many harbour resentment towards others without expressing it, rendering their grudge a solitary and futile affair.

This damaging dynamic underscores that the whimsical ego is not a companion of reason or compromise and is the antithesis of living the Two Truths.

Living the Two Truths is a matter of getting to know yourself and then appreciating that as a personal work-in-progress project, we should love ourselves enough not to make our progress through life any more challenging than it is.

Holding grudges, fostering and retaining negative emotions, and making overly harsh self-judgments are only a few examples of not getting to know ourselves sufficiently to prevent the emotional and mental harm derived from failing to love ourselves sufficiently.

Of course, many individuals embark on a spiritual journey in search of self.

These quests can lead them to ancient forests, sacred sites, meandering pilgrimages, and shamanic rituals.

Others immerse themselves in ancient scriptures, drink Ayahuasca, seek counsel from enlightened gurus, and pursue the spiritual equivalent of the Holy Grail.

All are noble pursuits, but, in the end, the answer to the quest is never a geography, an icon or a relic: it is always found within.

Whatever road someone takes to find their purpose, the starting and finishing point will always be the Two Truths. Learning to Love and Loving to Learn represent the core of your humanity and, thus, your connection to everyone Worldwide.

They are simple principles that encourage an uncomplicated and reliable way to nurture happiness, inclusion, forgiveness, personal growth, and wonderment about how extraordinary we can be as humans. Perhaps most importantly, they offer a firm foundation for loving ourselves unconditionally.

They are a way of appreciating that we have nothing to fear and can achieve more than we think possible.

Our pathway to a purposeful life begins and ends with the Two Truths. We come into the World with much to learn and much to love.

We end our days understanding two things: first, there remains much to learn, and second, we could have loved much more.

FINAL WORDS

As we come to the close of this little volume, I have a promise to make to you.

If you live the Two Truths (*genuinely embracing and living them*), you will experience new insights and a deeper understanding of your place in the cosmos and connectivity to all things living.

And what's more, you will enjoy the same inner peace, self-acceptance, and happiness that so many others have discovered when living the Two Truths.

In living the Two Truths, it is highly likely (*I speak from personal experience*) that you will stumble, get it wrong, become frustrated and occasionally fail. The ego, after all, is a difficult beast to slay.

On your quest, others may mock you, despitefully use you, and probably hurt you. And when that happens, it's not much fun.

However, this is a matter of standing in your truth, which is a feature of self-love, not self-abandonment.

You cannot afford to abandon yourself because doing so directly contradicts the need for self-love. Contentment, happiness and a purposeful life are directly proportional to how connected you are to living your truth, which is living your life and dreams on your terms.

After all, living your truth is a matter of doing those things that make you happy, confident, and connected to your heart.

And generally, there are five reasons we tend to abandon our truth, and they are:

- For someone's love
- For someone's acceptance and approval
- To keep the peace
- To maintain a state of harmony or balance
- Pretending to be other than who we are to gain love, acceptance or approval

Each of these reasons for self-abandonment can become habitual and sometimes push you into losing your identity. Indeed, if unregulated, you will find yourself either over-compromising, self-sacrificing, being needy or in a perpetual state of imbalance and unhappiness.

Self-abandonment has its roots in fear or ego. Where fear and ego exist, self-love and self-empowerment tend to be diluted, forgotten, or buried. Loving yourself sufficiently deeply overcomes fear and supports you in living your truth

So, if your truth is to challenge the status quo, protect the weak, offer constructive feedback, foster kindness, exit a toxic relationship, or expose the truth for others, then know that these are all acts of self-love.

Of course, living your truth can sometimes require courage, resilience, change, and breaking self-defeating habits, but these traits are inherent in all humans - although sometimes we feel we don't have them.

However, any disempowering view requires only one shift in perspective, and that is believing you deserve the best.

Or as the first-century scholar and sage Hillel the Elder eloquently explains:

> *"If I am not for myself, who will be for me?*
> *And being for myself, what am I? And if not now, when?"*

As you embrace living the Two Truths and enjoy the peace from standing in your truth, I want you to remember a couple of things. First, there is a time and season for others to embrace the Two Truths.

Only some people are ready to love or learn - and that's okay. It's a process for some and a matter of time for others. However, it shouldn't stop you from loving these folk because they need it, even if they do not know it.

Second, please remember the fundamental premise of the Two Truths: love is not conditional, and neither is learning. If you restrict either by making them conditional, you will lose the full benefit of loving and learning without condition.

However, learning to love and loving to learn takes work. Both require action and a commitment to taking 100% accountability for your life.

Living the Two Truths requires small steps and incremental gains. These steps require us to slow down, breathe, be more self-aware, and be more observant.

We must notice that tiny voice that consistently whispers to us to wrap our hearts and consciousness around the Two Truths so that we can do what is right and learn what is necessary.

The Two Truths foster all that is beautiful about humankind. Living them enlarges the soul, makes the world a better place and motivates us to rise above the mundane, mediocre, and profane. They offer a better way of living, connecting, elevating, achieving, loving and learning.

Even in isolation, the Two Truths can significantly enhance one's life. Consider the profound impact of fully embracing the first truth - learning to love unconditionally.

You would transcend the limitations of conditional love, navigate compromises more effectively, forge deeper connections with others, experience forgiveness more readily, and, most importantly, realise your inherent worth in deserving only the very best for yourself.

And what about the second truth?

Suppose you learned more about why you do and don't do certain things? Suppose you ditch fear and ego, learn how to be more open, find new ways to be creative, and discover new things about our diverse world. Imagine how you might grow and fall into new experiences.!

In isolation or together, the Two Truths are a powerful remedy for much of what ails our world.

If we are ever to understand and appreciate our cosmic worth, the worth of others, and the beauty of Mother Earth, then living the Two Truths is as necessary as the air we breathe.

As I conclude, I invite you to embark on a transformative journey. I challenge you to commit to living the Two Truths for a month, not just in theory but in every aspect of your life.

I assure you the results will be profound. Just as many of my clients have been pleasantly surprised, you, too, will discover new depths within yourself and experience a profound shift in your perspective.

I wish you good luck in bringing the Two Truths into your life. I hope your endeavours bring knowledge, creativity, wisdom, peace, happiness, meaningful relationships and, of course - much love.

Omnia Vincit Amor

TRUTH #1 - LEARN TO LOVE
Get more love in your life

Sometimes, we need a little dose of love to revive our spirits. And sometimes, nobody is nearby to wrap their arms around us, hug us, and let us know everything will be okay. By the way, giving and receiving hugs releases endorphins, reduces stress, and makes us feel connected. *(Be a hugger, is what I'm saying - it's good for your health!)*

Here are some suggestions to increase your love for yourself and others. Remember, love is a gift that multiplies when shared. So, don't keep something so good all to yourself. Share it generously and watch it spread joy and happiness.

- Send a bunch of flowers or a card unexpectedly to a friend or family member and imagine the smile on their face when they receive them.
- Show a kindness to a stranger – a smile, a conversation, a gift, some money.
- Watch a comedy movie. Your heart will appreciate the laughter.
- Treat yourself. Do something for yourself that you haven't done in a while – something you miss but really enjoy.
- Express your gratitude and love for someone. Let them know how they have positively influenced your life.
- Make someone feel important. Offer them praise, issue a high five, give them an award.
- List and celebrate your wonderful qualities and don't be shy: *everybody has them*. Wear these qualities with pride and be grateful they are part of you.

- Acknowledge and embrace your perfect imperfections. Big up your quirks, raise a flag to your weirdness, celebrate your inner and outer beauty, and fall in love with the amazing, unique human being that is you.
- Get into nature and calm your heart and mind. Immerse yourself in Mother Earth's beauty, after all – this is your home. Walk bare-foot on the ground, breath in fresh air, or listen to waves falling onto the beach. And while you are it - hug a tree.
- Interact with a furry friend. Stroke a cat, pat a dog, ride a horse, swim with a dolphin or share your feelings with a pet. They are the animal kingdom's experts in love because their love is unconditional - it is agape love.

TRUTH #2 - LOVE TO LEARN
Get more learning in your life

The author, Michael Gelb, suggests, "*Research shows that you begin learning in the womb and go right on learning until the moment you pass on. Your brain has a capacity for learning that is virtually limitless, which makes every human a potential genius.*"

In making incremental and meaningful steps towards our potential genius, our learning must start to make peace with the mirror and then see changes emanating from our hearts.

Here are some suggestions for you to increase your learning.

- Seek feedback from others about your character, behaviours, belief systems and values.
- Set, write down and commit to goals so they don't translate into pipe dreams.
- Step outside your comfort zone by learning something new, challenging some of the beliefs you hold or engage in something that makes you feel uncomfortable.
- Find a mentor, teacher or coach.
- Challenge your fears by asking yourself objective questions, getting support from others and changing your inner dialogue from fearing the worst to anticipating the best that can happen.
- Adapt and welcome change by harnessing a positive attitude and detaching from outcomes.
- Develop reading habit and keep a journal
- Embrace failure as a friend to your future self

GETTING AROUND TO SELF-HEALING

In today's fast-paced world, taking time for self-healing is essential for maintaining mental, emotional, and physical well-being.

Self-healing involves a variety of activities that promote relaxation, reduce stress, and enhance overall health.

Here are some effective activities you can incorporate into your daily routine to help you on your journey to self-heal.

Mindfulness and Meditation
Practicing mindfulness and meditation can significantly reduce stress and anxiety. Start with just five minutes a day, focusing on your breath and observing your thoughts without judgment. Apps like Headspace or Calm offer guided sessions for beginners.

Physical Exercise
Regular physical activity is crucial for both physical and mental health. Whether it's a brisk walk, yoga, or a workout at the gym, exercise releases endorphins, which are natural mood lifters. Aim for at least 30 minutes of moderate exercise most days of the week.

Healthy Eating
Nutrition plays a vital role in self-healing. Incorporate a balanced diet rich in fruits, vegetables, whole grains, and lean proteins. Avoid processed foods and excessive sugar, as they can negatively affect your mood and energy levels.

Journaling
Writing down your thoughts and feelings can be incredibly therapeutic. Journaling helps you process emotions, identify patterns in your thinking, and set goals for personal growth. Try to write for at least ten minutes each day.

Creative Expression

Engaging in creative activities such as painting, drawing, music, or crafting can be a powerful form of self-healing. Creativity allows you to express emotions and can be a great way to distract yourself from stressors.

Nature Walks

Spending time in nature has been shown to reduce stress and improve mood. Take regular walks in a park, forest, or by the sea. The fresh air and natural surroundings can help you feel more grounded and relaxed.

Adequate Sleep

Quality sleep is essential for healing. Aim for 7-9 hours of sleep per night. Establish a regular sleep routine, create a relaxing bedtime environment, and avoid screens before bed to improve sleep quality.

Social Connections

Building and maintaining strong social connections can greatly enhance your well-being. Spend time with family and friends, join a club, or participate in group activities that interest you. Sharing experiences and feelings with others fosters a sense of belonging and support.

Reading and Learning

Reading books, whether fiction or non-fiction, can be an excellent way to relax and gain new perspectives. Learning new skills or hobbies keeps your mind active and engaged, contributing to your overall sense of purpose and fulfilment.

Self-Compassion

Finally, practice self-compassion. Treat yourself with the same kindness and understanding you would offer a friend. Acknowledge your imperfections and mistakes without harsh self-criticism. Accepting yourself as you are is a crucial step towards self-healingd

WORKSHOPS

As you can imagine, I know how important the Two Truths are to personal growth and the accomplishment of personal happiness and peace.

And so, you might like to know I conduct workshops and 1-1 sessions throughout the year that help people bring the Two Truths into their lives.

If you would like to find out more, please go to:
http://www.twotruthsoneworld.com/resources

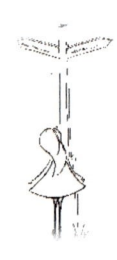

OTHER BOOKS BY STEVE

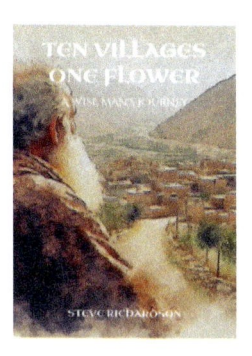

Ten Villages - One Flower - *A Wise Man's Journey*
Follow the footsteps of a wise teacher as he travels through his community, sharing wisdom and timeless lessons about topics as diverse as grief, love, and loneliness. **Ten Villages – One Flower** is a beautifully illustrated exploration of wisdom, simplicity, and the transformative power of universal truths.

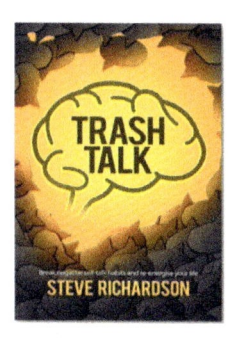

Trash Talk
30-40 trillion cells make up the human body When these cells are exposed to negative thoughts, they become damaged, and we become susceptible to health and emotional problems. Learn how to recognise and combat these the *Trash Talk* in your head.

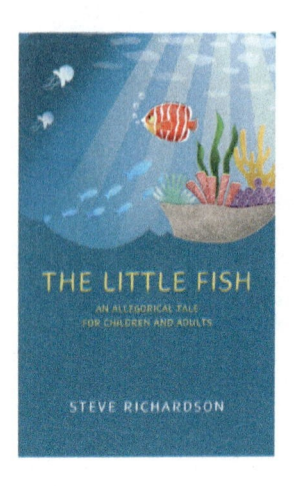

The Little Fish

During a violent storm a small silver fish is cast ashore on a beach. While lying on the shore, contemplating his life and fate, he is visited by three messengers.

Each visitor shares important messages and truths about the world in which the little fish now finds himself.

He learns valuable lessons about himself and how, if he were returned to the ocean, he would live a different life. The Little Fish is a heart-warming allegorical story for children and adults alike, that explores friendships, perspective, regret and transformation.

ABOUT THE AUTHOR

Steve Richardson, a Clinical Hypnotherapist, Humanistic Therapist, life and career coach, and Reiki Master, is a passionate optimist and humanist who believes in the inherent greatness of every individual.

His latest book, *Two Truths - One World*, is a transformative guide that encourages readers to embrace two essential truths for a purposeful and harmonious life.

Outside of his professional endeavours, Steve finds solace in the Scottish Highlands, where he enjoys wild camping and climbing.

He also has a love for creative pursuits, regularly participating in flash fiction competitions, solving cryptic crosswords, and pursuing his lifelong quest to find the perfect recipe for vanilla ice cream.

Printed in Great Britain
by Amazon